me, her, him

Sarah Francis

Presentation by *BookLeaf Publishing*

Web: www.bookleafpub.com

E-mail: info@bookleafpub.com

ISBN: 9789357743952

First edition 2023

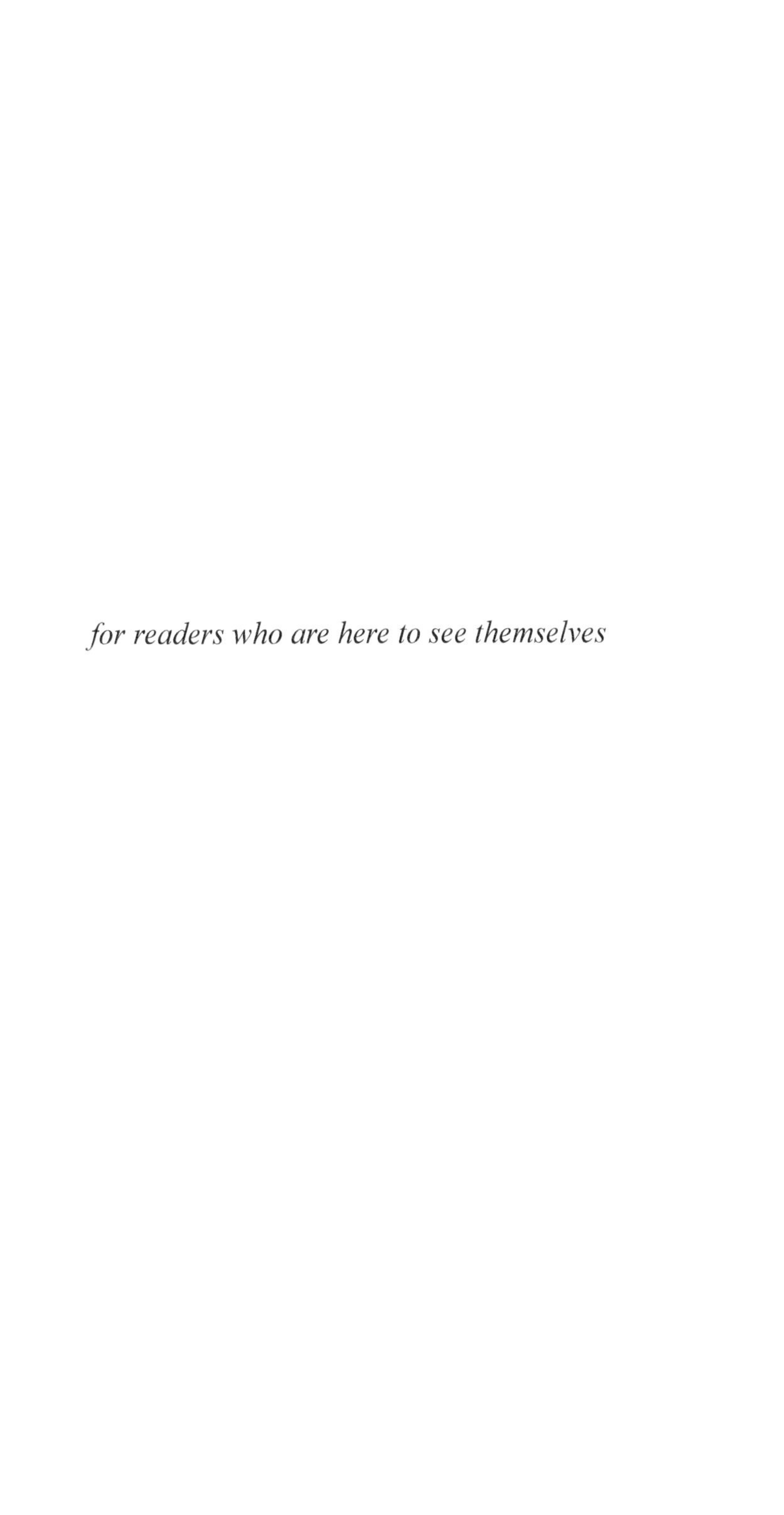

for readers who are here to see themselves

PREFACE

i'm no frost or tennyson,

and far from hemingway

but i've got a story to tell

and words to be read

for the heart and soul.

- Sarah Francis

drowning

the river of tears has flowed for so long

that i lie each night in an ocean

that drowns me

with each breath i take

in order to survive.

time

every second,

every minute,

every hour,

every day,

every week,

every month,

every year,

makes me question how i will survive until the very end.

unhappiness

have i committed too many sins in this world to
be happy?

have i done too many wrongs that nothing seems
to turn out right?

have i wished on the wrong stars in the sky?

have i not blown out the candles just right?

why does it feel like i will never smile again?

survival

how do i survive?

do i play pretend?

do i put on a mask?

do i bury everything i have ever been taught?

for a lifetime of happiness?

hopeless

that wishing well

is dry as a bone

for all the desires

of my heart.

the sky is pitch black

with no shooting star

in sight

for i have wishes

that will never be made.

there are no

fortune cookies

predicting a future

of peace and prosperity.

conceal

i'm a professional pretender

that majored in lies and cover-ups.

i stroll the streets

with a mask at night.

now all that's left of me

is scars and a broken heart.

compass

north,

south,

east,

west,

in which direction do i find myself?

maiden name,

married name,

which do i belong?

needs

dear little queer me.

here's a hug.

here's a hand.

here's a safety net.

here's the comfort you always longed for.

here's the family you always dreamed of having.

here's an eraser for your past.

here's a rainbow with a pot of gold for all that
may come to be.

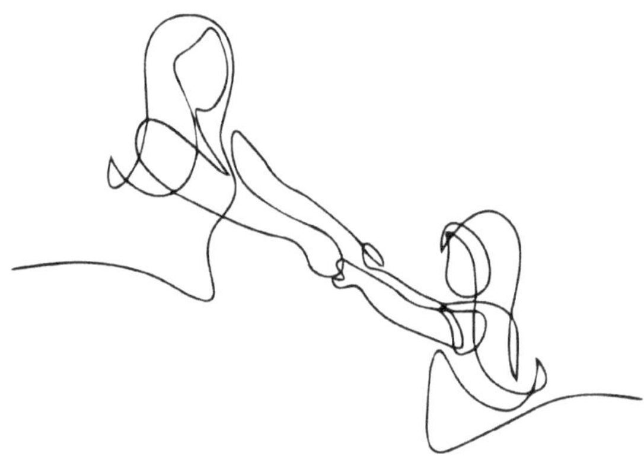

gender

female

girl

lady

gal

madame

senora

sweetheart

dame

i love them all.

royalty

the jewels

are aligned

for this queen-on-queen action

but

there's no need

for a crown

to call you mine.

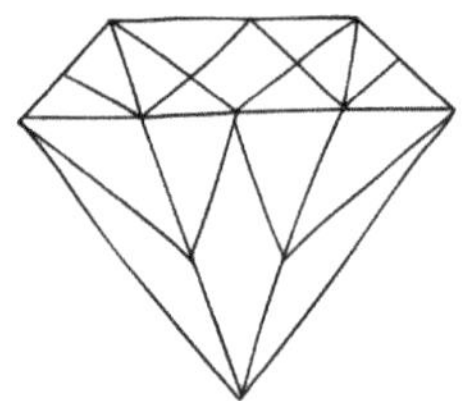

jackpot

it was everything good,

winning the lottery,

caviar and champagne,

a dream vacation,

when my lips met yours.

faster

the fan spun faster.

my heart beat faster.

i wanted you in me faster.

but, the truth is

i wanted the time to slow down

to savor the moment with you.

attraction

introvert

extrovert

feminine

masculine

blond

brunette

opposites

attract.

bliss

she dreams of the day

she can lie in her arms

and it is heavenly bliss.

no one will gruffle.

everyone will approve.

it will be a dream come true.

mourning

i mourn the life i wish i had,

the one where rainbows filled every horizon,

and your presence

was my pot of gold.

the one where happiness was bountiful,

and you were my saving grace.

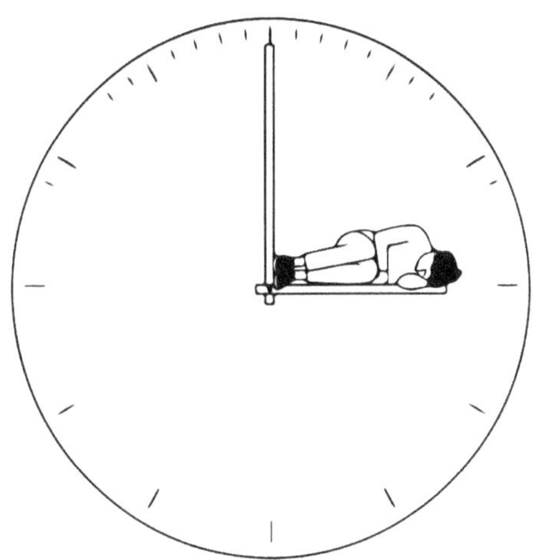

pride

why can't every month be june?

where rainbows dance in our eyes,

and pride is shown in our smiles.

where flags are flown for all to see,

and parades are held for you and me.

why can't every month be june?

complete

it was hard for me

to catch my breath

from the pulsating heartbeat

you left me with

after we made love.

the sweat on the sheets

felt like our skin

had just cried

a river of tears

because we were so happy

to have found each other.

embracing you meant that i

had found my missing puzzle piece.

sharing

i want to share

the shoes and clothes.

i want to share

my inner thoughts with you.

i want to share

my bed with your body.

i want to share

a lifetime with you.

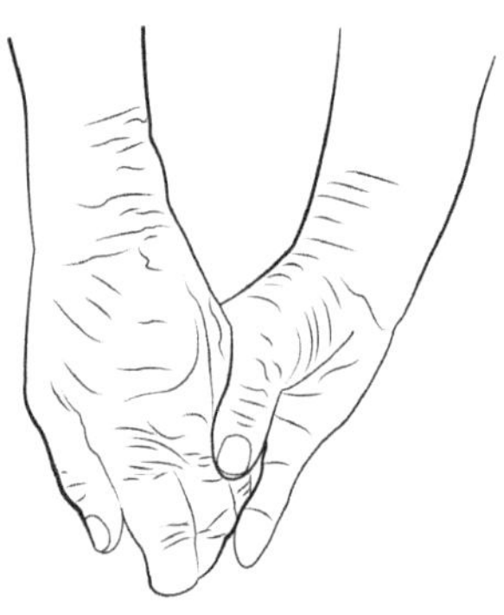

you

when my heart is beating out of my chest,

you are the cause of it.

when i am hot and bothered,

you are the cause of it.

when i die of a broken heart,

you will be the cause of it.

longing

i long
for the mornings that are spent waking up beside
you.
i long
for the nights that are spent falling asleep next to
you.
i long
for your scent to engulf my senses.
i long
for your arms to hold me tight.
i long
for the heat of your body to keep me warm.
i long
for my name to escape your lips to confirm that
i am yours.

awakening

i was dead inside

until you

touched me,

tasted me,

tantalized me with your tongue.

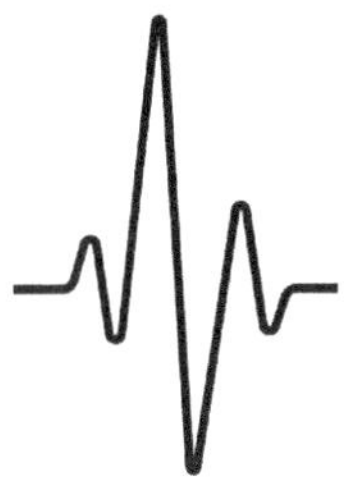